BEAST BOOK

BEAST BOOK

Michael Gessner

BlazeVOX [books]

Buffalo, New York

BEAST BOOK by Michael Gessner

Published by BlazeVOX [books]

Printed in the United States of America

Book design by Geoffrey Gatza
Cover: 'Beaver and Panther' from *The Aberdeen Bestiary*, c. 12th century

First Edition
ISBN: 978-1-60964-002-6
Library of Congress Control Number 2010906697

BlazeVOX [books]
303 Bedford Ave
Buffalo, NY 14216

Editor@blazevox.org

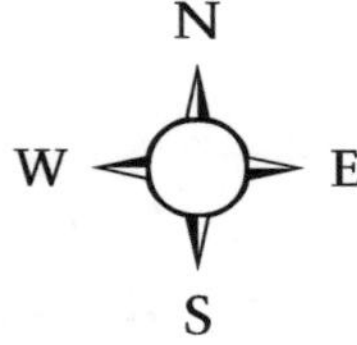

publisher of weird little books

BlazeVOX [books]

blazevox.org

2 4 6 8 0 9 7 5 3 1

B X

Grateful acknowledgment is made to those publications in which some of these poems first appeared:

10x3: "After Hours, a Consolation," "Mantichore Speaks," "Parthenogenesis," "Purity, a Sylph," "Hoodoos"
Amaranth Review: "Confession to a Girl"
American Literary Review: "Rites of Spring"
Buffalo Spree Magazine: "Ineffable Conversations"
Byline: "Canticle, Poet-Anima"
The Journal of The American Medical Association, (JAMA): "Gifts"
Poem: (University of Alabama Press): "White Doors"
Wisconsin Review: "Description of Sea Life," "Other Acts"

For Martin Turner

1948 – 2010

CONTENTS

"And I saw one of his heads as it were wounded to death; and his deadly wound was healed: and all the world wondered after the beast."

—Book of Revelation
Apocalypse 13:3

"Ask now the beasts, and they shall teach thee;
And the fowls on the air, and they shall teach thee;
Or speak to the earth, and it shall teach thee;
And the fishes of the sea shall declare unto thee."

—Job 12:7, 8

"All things are poison . . . . only the dose permits something not to be poisonous."

—Paracelsus

"The world is better, the more things it contains."

—Arthur O. Lovejoy

BEAST BOOK

Hercules capturing Cerberus, Three-Headed Dog of Death, Beham, 1545

BEAST HANDLER

On the coldest nights
I take down my dead father's sweater
that warms me more than wool,
& reminds me of the search
for ancestors, how Mathias,
the banker, and Boeckler, the accountant
found my father's family
in the old church records in Würzburg.

We were descended from the patriarch
Conrad & his noble clan, that German Pliny,
—this would explain my love of mountains
& higher altitudes, flowers perhaps—
whose family was from Nuremberg,
north of Zürich, & his descendent,
Salomon, author of *Daphnis*, & other pastoralia,
a modern Theocritus, according to Mary Collyer,
translator of his *Death of Abel.*

That may be, Boeckler says,
may be by cousins, & swirls one hand
above his head to suggest the mix

of time & progeny, geography & time,
but My Kale, *your* people were . . .
he clicks his fingers for the word,
looks at Mathias who looks a bit sad
& confused . . . were . . . how is it said,
beast handlers. Silence.
He clarifies: your people were wanderers.
They were *servants to the animals.*

Silence. More clarification: they did not
serve *people.* No they did not
protect the prince-bishop in Würzburg,
or care for the well-to-do in Bad Königshofen.

In Wettringen, for example, there is
your namesake, Michael Gessner,
b. 1732 (the year your mother's family
plotted for independence in Ireland,)
and who was—here it is in
the record—a handler of beasts.
We know this from the house number
—families may be traced for centuries—
the house number remains the same
& all who live there register yearly
in the archives, they must record births,
deaths, employment, & from this man, My Kale,
we follow his family to Saal,
then to Kleinbardorf where your
grandfather was born & taken to St. Ägidius
—the baptismal font was built in 550—
& the names of crusaders are carved
on marble scrolls that flank the altar,
(your family is not among them,)

& in this region, farm implements
have been unearthed dating to 9,000 B.C.E.
So you see, your people did not stay
in one place very long. They were not
like the others. Mathias & Boeckler smile.
They concur.

Thus & forever after, I am called
by those enduring residents
of the village, Michael-the-shepherdman-
from-America. For them, this clarifies everything.

But the beasts have changed.
They are no longer ox & cow, lamb & sheep,
or objects of moral illustration only,
they have become the forms of our condition,
more homunculi than beasts,
the omnivore of fecundity,
the headless creature of loss,
the twin brutes of self-contempt & loathing,
the heart-eaters, carnivores of conscience,
to rise above ourselves, to find
the noble moment, this too
is in the menagerie,
along with the beast of renown & desolation,
and the greatest beast of all,
the angel-beast of oblivion.

And still they require attention
& that is fixed,
& for the fairer creatures,
the sylphs that attend them,
& summer's etherea,
the vagaries of perspective,
the fatigue of magnanimity,
compassion & dissolution,
dissolution of the compassionate,

the stockyards of envy & contempt,
the indefinable maw
of misshaped intention,
the beast of the marsh
& indecision, phantom hooves,
& conspiracy, the consequences
of surrender & discovery,
their attendants, a royal train
of endless obligation,
& the responsibility of responsibility
itself, the contempt for moderation
& the contempt for excess,
feeding in meadows of speculation,
I am what the villagers say,
a wanderer trying to find his people,
in my father's cloth,
waving an airy crook
among elusive meadows.

Caspar Schott, *Physica Curiosa*, 1662,
Clerical Beasts, Bishop & Monk
with two tritons.

CANTICLE,

Poet-Anima

It was a strange awakening
that moved from place to place
staring at itself
like the first thought of the body.

The birds stood on the roof,
waited in the rain
& belonged to no house.
There was cold music

in the spinal column
from the city & from the plain,
shuddering at dawn and at sunset,
prosperous as one thought

I was Paris

& I was the Serengeti

A SUITE

for the Four Primary Animals of Passion

Greed: Gold heart. In the condominium of luxury,
among overstuffed pillows
there is the heart of pity & fear,
the black heart from which all of us
suffer. Emptiness. Something was taken
from us & cannot be recovered.
It is the source of all aggression.

Lust: Red heart. When dancing with another
I dance also with myself & what is now
mandatory, passes, only to return
again; the compelling *entré* that takes
us up those weary steps
to the event which notes its passing
even as it is passing.

Beauty: Blue heart. The sum of the pageant
& the parade is always the same & there
is no place to turn once ruin is understood;
that it is wished for by others,
the admirers, & that it will arrive no matter
what, & just as blessings rise in favor,
suffering grows too & follows behind, disguised.

Permanence: Invisible heart. The condition is irreducible.
I am with you always & was never
a thing outside itself, zoo or carousel,
but for you, & all the others, after you
had gone, & all that was before
anything arrived, before movement
was noticed, or heart's beating.

ACCOMPLICES

They seem compatible,
companions even, honor
& revenge, for instance,
camouflaged in the park,
& the triplets; vulgarity, spectacle
& self-promotion, with a singular
bright face, another example
of the existence of the polycephalic
found in most species; deception & love,
(all kinds,) purity with its double,
loathing, or deformity & justice,
or those bearing the soft down
of agreement & conciliation, the politicos,
& the most genuine, the contemptuous,
bearing quills, (porcupine, hedgehog,
Echidna, spiny rat,) or those stingers
on the webbed feet of the platypus,
or those in the zoo
of lofty principle, & their offspring,
ridicule & remorse, & when all
is shaken & then abandoned,
when torment has ceased
for some other thing,
there is disengagement
from all discord, a settlement,
the vacant stare,
& there are always
the special ones, selections made
in the dead of night by criteria
unknown to the public, the cohorts
we find so often in manufacturing,
tourism, commerce, fair trade,

a political model, like oil, squirting
out of the machine, arrogance & cynicism
attending a luncheon with platitudes,
& across the expanses of the great
deserts, there are caravans
of the commonplace, with creed
& cause & flag,
throngs of newborns
in a mall nursery
as if they were their own
family crying in unison,
& our belongings
given to coteries; water circles
invading others & thus, never
entirely ourselves, unless left
to the undistinguished presence
of that form which never had identity
but which we know is ours & ours
alone, belonging like another body
equal & invisible with our own.

WHITE DOORS

Always there was the dumb look of animals,
the black and stationary eyes
of the field mouse, rabbit, or sleek ferret
fixed on nothing, or on destruction.

Still they were vulnerable
as in their movements, clumsy,
or swift with elegance & desire,

imagined spirits who could not speak,
quiet as innocence walking alone
or the sea turning inside

the sea around the summer pavilion
at the end of the pier where the water
tugs at the pilings to dispose
vagrant, vendor, or financier.

The sea, clumsy in its pulling
as a dumb lover trying
to own & be owned
by the creature of desire.

THE NEXT GREAT EXTINCTION

for Wendell Berry

Something grim is about to happen.
We sense it. O it is in the air.
The weather's wary; the birds skittish.
We are losing tundra at an alarming rate.

We have lived with one Apocalypse
or another from earliest memory,
something we knew before our birth,
locked-in like a spirochete.

Surviving the next great extinction
is something we must plan for
now. By saving other species
we will save the planet and save

ourselves. Even schoolchildren know
this. Global warming destroys habitat.
Black carbon is shrinking the polar cap.
Flagship species, caribou & white bear,

arctic fox & Emperor penguin will be lost.
And down south, the clownfish of the coral
reefs & the gentle Koala are leaving & will never
return. Where are their replacements?

Will we recognize them? More loss.
The new extinction will be the worst.
Number six. Talk about global terror.
Oceans will swallow seacoasts.

(Did greenhouse gases, China's coal,
overpopulation, or jet fuel sacrifice
the fair Marrella, or the briny Anomalocaris
caught a half-billion years ago in Burgess' shale?)

Plants & animals will perish in untold numbers.
We will not be able to see the sun.
Scientists cannot work fast enough;
they need everyone's help.

The dying animal does not see
tonight's lightning all about him.
It will take ten million years to recover
from the destruction. Still, we will not

be entirely out of the woods.
Behind it all, the planet continues to cool.
We cannot reverse this, or argue
with the passions of the molten core.

As the magnetosphere diminishes, so too
does our protection from solar flares
& radiation. More polarity reversals.
But there's always the cooling . . . . the cooling . . . .

We could be Pluto. Cosmic extinctions
may follow. These may be black holes,
dark matter, or some unknown and insurmountable
Thing, so we really need to plan ahead.

Who wants to float out past the farthest moon
where there is nothing but cosmic cold,
drifting for a billion years,
hoping for a radio wave, a companion, another rock?

In the meantime maybe we will be
saved by a rapture, or space travel, or virtual
animation when another self will get
a second chance, or The Great Contact

when extraterrestrials return
to check our progress, and we can pose
with the long lost, compare appendages,
have a real reunion, make family albums.

TESLA'S PIGEON

In the Hagia Sophia
I saw Tesla's white pigeon
circling upward
in the Great Dome
of consciousness, where everything
is said to hover,
where recollections dim,
& joined her in her radiance
like Zeus, whispering over & over
that I was him, Nikola, her lover.

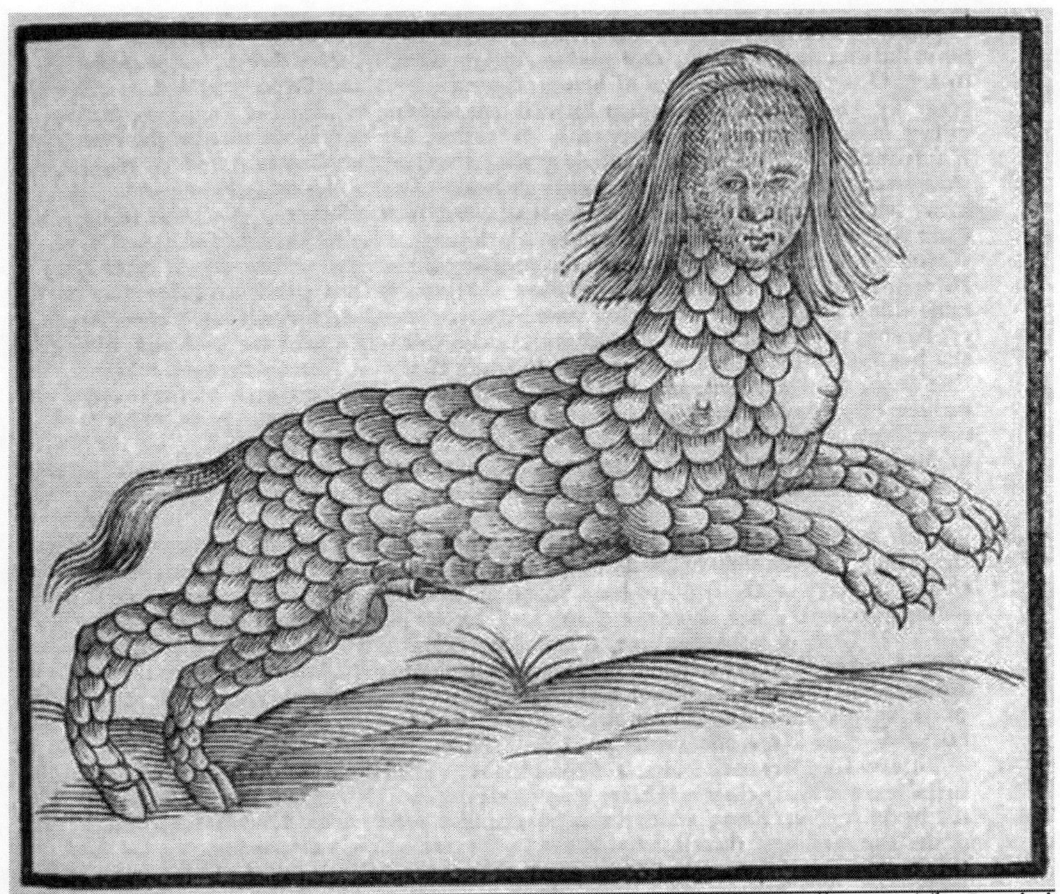

The Lamia, from *The Historie of Foure-Footed Beastes*, Edward Topsell, 1607. The Lamia is said to hiss & entice men by the beauty of face and breasts, then slays them, as she slays her children.

HEART-EATER

The tip of the Forest Elephant's tail,
(adult swampgorth, or flying chimera,)
is spade-shaped; red heart/black heart.
It is the heart of the Lamia,
that Queen of Shark hearts,

tail-tip, or cartilage-shape of the stingray's
hood, the water's pterodactyl,
who feeds on adolescent love,
eating the exposed heart

& transforming it to its root,
the killing shaft, the serrated pike
that shoots through the diver's skin.

It is excess,
a dose greater than needed or good;
heart eating heart.

HOODOOS

The Hoodoos of history
are almost always deformed,
& deformities matter;
Pope trying to tie his shoelaces,
Byron gone skating,
Lincoln at midnight
skulking about the Old Soldiers'
Home looking for some wounded boy.

They are the twisted totems of tabloids,
on an imaginary island, each standing
outside a tent of their belongings,
where only beetles enter,
while the collective mind is attracted
to the curious figures of central casting,
Seneca slumping with his jewels & pinky ring,
beckoning Vice from an overstuffed chair,
and to other front-page headlines:

Chatterton complains to friendly apothecary
of rodent infestation.

Woolf consults Ophelia on streams & stones.

Poe in mirror discusses effects of Laudanum
& other hallucinogens with Coleridge.

Hale climbs Mt. Palomar
to see the edge of the universe
holding hands with neurasthenic elf.

Lewis on bended knee, proposes to Alice,
age 11, promising an abundance of toys
as wedding gifts, "enough for a life."

Plath & Sexton debate nature of gases,

& Tesla meets Hughes in secret vault
for talks on hygiene
& that death ray designed
to disinfect the mysophobe.

The geology of adoration
must be disfigured. No stone left unmarked,
a hammer will be taken to the Hoodoo
every time. We cannot tolerate perfection
for long. We must find its fatal flaw
which is the flaw of the fallen.

Victim gossip and victim art
converse while beetles inventory the tents,
& the great Hoodoos of history
stand bowed & broken. Even for those
who have no greatness to give, they have
work to do if only in sharing their own
victimizations, before the aliens
arrive once again, ghastly,
gnashing their spiked teeth
out of the green lumps growing from our backs.

HISTORY

You woke
terrified, you said
because you could not
remember my face.
But that is history
I said, consoling you,
tremulous creature,
longest love, & cannot be
erased.

FECUNDITY

Arises midmorning,
a coil from a shell
to become almost anything,
to spread out across the sky,
turn outward, become another
world beckoning & unseen,
but chooses instead
to walk the beach again
with a rhythm
like warm wind,
or on the prowl
until exhausted, spent
then settles down
like fat in a pot.

Androgynous fecundity figure from *Istorica Descrizione de tre regni Congo, Matamba et Angola*, 1687 by Giovanni Antonio Cavazzi, Capuchin friar & missionary.

THE DODO AND THE SWAN

The death of Anna Pavlova was the birth of Ophelia.
The persistence of the nimbus of Christ
cannot be distinguished from the aura of Napoleon Bonaparte
& ambition, given too much from the start
runs into walls with armfuls of ideals.

In a flash she was here & in a flash she was gone.
The fragile hand that held the silver feathers
is in the hand of morning where all the deaths are
& in the hand of morning
assuming any understanding
becomes pitifully disorganized—

Observe: the dodo & the swan.

Anna Pavlova's *pas seul* is accompanied
by jackals laughing into tomorrow—
(easy to understand why 'Divine Sarah' kept reminiscent roses
& love letters line the coffin in which she napped.)

The best of acts are mawkish
as the look of crippled birds,
(& as for them what might we expect now, or ten centuries hence?)

The greater the gift, less justice in the giving
& in cruelty worse than the cripple
strapped to his chair turning himself
in silver circles now or ten centuries hence.

Death: you dignify pity.

Behind the warehouse, among the wrecked cars
is a nest of dead birds & nightly
across the sky expectation sprawls
like the skeleton of wings.

Only what is real is permanent:
The death of Anna Pavlova is the birth of Ophelia.

THE THOUSAND CONSOLATIONS

Notes on a New Year

It is the time of year when temple bells are rung.
They are heavy, & black with pollution,
with dragons, & snakes intertwined.

There is a gong for garrulity,
one for sarcasm, another for pride.
There is a gong for greed.
For vanity there is a gong.
Deceit & fraudulence, there are gongs for these.
There is another for sinister calculation, & one for regret.
There is a gong for every sorrow of the human heart.
Gong over gong, they echo over each other, a doubling,
as the old gong fades into the new
until the Buddha bells recant
all 108 defilements.

Then silence.
It is the New Year.
Now is the Future of Things.

In the Future of Things
I will not want.
There will be no Valley of Death.
Those whom I love will not suffer.
I will never be alone.

MATCHING

The current of air
    that sweeps cold across
    my deck one morning is this.
Or say, a world
brighter than my own
floats to mind,

    and I have stepped outside
the self & into another
zone occupied
    with foreign sensations only,
    like the mourning dove about the house
    flown inside.

The Forstteufel, forest devil, or Satyr with Pendulous Breasts from *Historiae Animalium*, Conrad Gessner, 1558

EVENING OF A SATYR

It is the classical hour on cable,
the girl in the off-white tattered dress
coiled on center stage in blue darkness
has become herself faun & afternoon.
Bluer shadows move over drapes & floor,
like the flute's wood-notes through which she weaves,

a reaction to displace the evening
meeting, hers was the form she had assumed
for nothing more than this, uncoiling
herself upward in a spiral, fingering space
for some transparent film, in pursuit
of essence; how we judge the body's worth.

CONSCIENCE

(*Satyr to Nymph*)

Conscience sleeps with one eye open,
a notorious omnivore
consuming everything in its path,
good intentions, trust, the ultimate
relationship. A gaping orifice
it will eat it all, and praise itself
with sickness.

Today it feeds on grief & pride,
and tomorrow it denies itself
which creates regret & longing
for its inwardness. Like BASILISK
it can kill with a glance.
When it has achieved its highest point,
it collapses, & waits for itself,
a victim with one eye open.

Basilisk, from *Ephemerides,* Georg Wedel, 1672

MEMORANDUM TO MR. CREELEY

Who Once Dissuaded Youth
from The Pursuit of Poetry

from Mythos

Bob, you old Beat, must you claw
at your one good eye? Must you?
Like the fallen ostrich who kicks himself
trying to get up, kicks until he kicks
himself to death, is this what it has come to?

The ostrich which has the largest eye
of any animal, the bird of Paré, said to stare
at her eggs until they cracked, and tonight
among these chicks, it is yours.

If you wish is to be
like the ancient seers, like Tiresias,
then do not fail yourself,
become blind, do not remain as you are,
one-eyed, & half right.

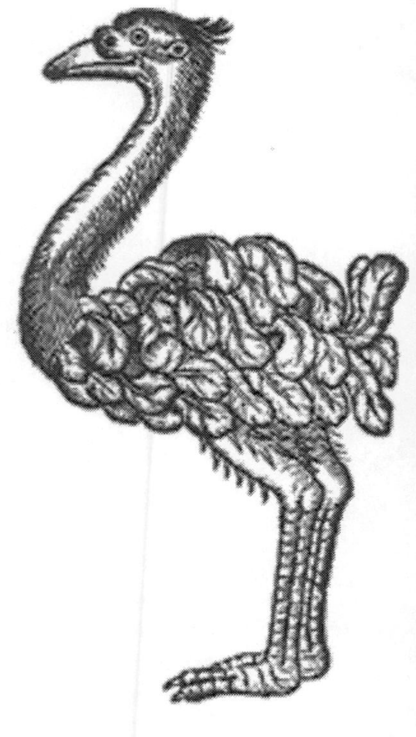

One-eyed Ostrich, from *Des Monstres,* Ambroise Paré, 1573-1585?

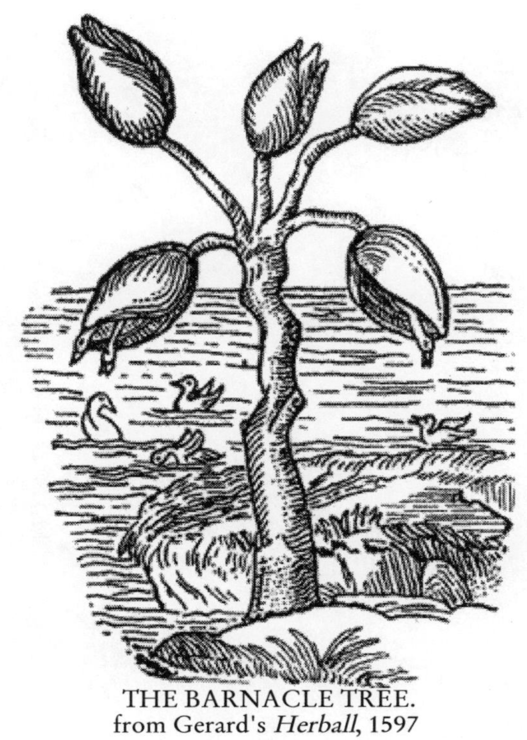

THE BARNACLE TREE.
from Gerard's *Herball*, 1597

Nature produces [Bernacae] against Nature in the most extraordinary way. They are like marsh geese but somewhat smaller. They are produced from fir timber tossed along the sea, and are at first like gum. Afterwards they hang down by their beaks as if they were a seaweed attached to the timber, and are surrounded by shells in order to grow more freely. Having thus in process of time been clothed with a strong coat of feathers, they either fall into the water or fly freely away into the air. They derived their food and growth from the sap of the wood or from the sea, by a secret and most wonderful process of alimentation. I have frequently seen, with my own eyes, more than a thousand of these small bodies of birds, hanging down on the sea-shore from one piece of timber, enclosed in their shells, and already formed. They do not breed and lay eggs like other birds, nor do they ever hatch any eggs, nor do they seem to build nests in any corner of the earth.

Topographica Hiberniae, Giraldus Cambrensis, 1187

BARNACLE GEESE

A TRIALOGUE

Cast:

Dionysian Goose
Apollonian Goose
B.V.M. as Dame Consolation

Dame Consolation:

You are as a see-saw, one on each side
balancing the other. Do not hit
the ground.

Dionysian Goose:

The ground is necessary. That is how
we know ourselves.

Apollonian Goose:

You make things impossible.
I seek the noble moment.

Dame Consolation:

O wise goose,
you are wise to know the moment
you seek.

Dionysian Goose:

You take sides.

Dame Consolation:

I am the fulcrum.
You are like Juvenal's dark swans,
a rarity, & you, Dion, have come home
with rumpled feathers, bloodshot eyes,

& Appo, by contrast, is not much better
off, far too rigid, where you are far too
lax, & for regret, you are both the same.

You need a third in this pond, or more,
it is not enough to be a bimorph,
there must be mythic geese as well,
there is always room for others,
knowing water & land & not so much
of each cannot be fatal.

Dionysian Goose:

But that would not be *me.*

Apollonian Goose:

Nor I.

Dame Consolation:

In a state of placid reserve
neither imperious or stoic,

(but a drachm of each)
a truly silicon goose,
a golden goose, may glide by
unnoticed, like silent Polyphony,
even when entering that solemn realm
of despair where the wounded lay
unattended, where they have gone
to die alone while Enigma,
open-mouthed, entranced
by the gymnasts of hybrid forms,
in the carnival of animals
among the maintainers that are
neither contributors, as you Apollonian,
or absorbers, as you Dionysian,
but a synthesis, like the politicians
of the Galápagos, among penguins
& petrels, & the Blue-footed Booby,
the Guayaquil Squirrel, & all manner of seals,
among the polymorphs, Darwin's finches,
there with Mythos the loneliest lover,
was the birth of the Barnacle Goose.

Apollonian Goose: We need a Hegelian goose.

Dionysian Goose: No, we need a Marquis de Sade Goose.

Dionysian Goose & Apollonian Goose (in unison):

We have combined to become another,
to survive the great beast of oblivion
& we were thus from the beginning,
& only you saw the difference
between us.

CONTRIBUTORS

from *De Monstris*, Fortunio Liceti, (1577-1657)
Cephalic Types, a Variorum

PARTHENOGENESIS

from Hydra

CLONING is not new
& has been observed repeatedly
in the formicine ant, the scorpion,
Hammerhead shark; in Flora,
the Komodo dragon, who gave
a virgin birth to eight on Christmas,
& in the human species;
in Agnes of God, St. Clare
of the Flowering Rock, and Mother Mary,
all reproduced without earthly mates,
although pregnancy is a hardship without an accomplice,

& occurs in other conditions as well,
in suspicion, or fear, these are communicable
& repeat themselves in others,
& once they assume shape, continue.
In this way are they given life,
go on the prowl, like MANTICHORE.
When they recur, come home, so to speak,
they may take up with others,
a synthesis, and it is how we account
for our changelings, our other selves
like the voice we cannot quite recognize
but must search out, join, to become
what they are.

Seven-Headed Hydra, *De Pescium et Aquatilium Animantum Natura*, Conrad Gessner, 1558

MANTICHORE SPEAKS

HYDRA, you overrate me
& I am nothing like you imagine.
I cannot use my teeth as arrows,
or change into other creatures,
nor do I have your impossible head
for things.

It is not true; I do not consume
carousels of sylphs
like white flies about some food source.
The villagers gave me extra powers
from frenzy & fear. I offer the certainty
of horror, night-stories around fire pits,
& caprice. You are no match
for me, tho' I stay away from water,
the vipers, magic trees,
& live for what men see in me,
what they most admire in themselves,
vigor, gallantry.

The Mantichore, from *Historiae Animalium*

SYLPHS

In essence, the SYLPH is a wisp
of air, deliquescent, sometimes
colored by reflections of sun
glinting off particles of ozone
& oxide in the troposphere
which is their habitat, & may seem
as slips of pale pink, or pale gold,
become opalescent,
or never appear to appear at all.

They are simple presences only.
When not resting in thermal hammocks,
or attracted to the pleasance
that emanates from musings,
they are taken up by GUSTS
& blown about, or they may drift
in the trailings of clouds,
or descend; breath of bee
& butterfly, turn white
& float as Caddis do, or dally
in the vibrations made
from hummingbirds' wings.
They are a confusion
to HYDRA & MANTICHORE.

INNOCENCE has named them;
Chance & Gesture. Frailty.
Glimpse &Vision. Purity.
Paradise.

In dissolution, wind & water
conspire to replenish another,
unknown to the thing itself,
& thus the SYLPH is parthenogenic
& this accounts for the continuation
of their simple presence,
these wisps of air, with or without
color, or direction.

GLITTERATI

We are driven by our fascinations.
Glossiness gliding down 5th Avenue,
the imagined life of adulation,
model, saint, club killer.

Arrested by surface attractors,
the impulse is irresistible,
it is what takes the debutante
to the tattoo parlor.

It is obedience to the magic image.
We are ruled by sparkling things,
like Marilyn in silver lamé
& Arthur with all his shining honors.

The moment of conception was born itself
under the mirrored ball in the dance palace,
replayed in chains of bubbles in countless flutes
of champagne, luminous & effervescent.

The glitterati, hunched over a table,
share the first glint of revolution,
it is all about them.
They toast—a sparkling future.

THEORY OF CONSPIRACY

The conspirators are all around us.
It is true. This is not mental illness,
say paranoia. It is not thinking
about our thinking that makes their threat real.

They are concocting the next illusion
as we speak, & belong to a secret society.
No one knows why. They will
promise you anything.

The conspirators are responsible for the way we see
the world. For example, they tell us
we must personalize them
when they are not personal at all.

The society works in unison; we see this
clearly in our aspirations—visiting
the world itself, or achieving some measure
of prominence as when we were

young and full of electrical impulses & always
hungry. They feed on this. The agents
are everywhere. Informants pay.
Everyone, it seems, is doing their work now.

INEFFABLE CONVERSATIONS

All right Leonardo
so the hairs of the ox are alive
& the scrolls of animal skins
sense the words written on them.

Do the morning leaves
above the buried dead
hold an unaccountable breath?
Is the current moment round?

Is this what you mean?

Enough for Einstein's universe
to reside on a curved plane,
what ancients knew in the figure eight
on its side, seductive as an expanding
polyverse of sense, an evening out on the town,
Odalisque reclining on her lounge.

Robins' eggs in the pockets of boys,
broken wheels & grain silos in fields,
spires that vainly exclaim their point,
cathedral vaults, the human forehead, planets,
& Leonardo, even the shape of your eyes,

this geometry does not surprise,
or for this, we search for a symmetry
not our own, another longing to be told.

THIS WAS AN EVENING

from Spectre, a Sylph

This was an evening that will remain
in the mind of memory
itself, will stay like a ghost image
through rain. It was determined to be so
from the beginning.

The shelves of clouds with gilt ledges,
the volumes of gray in shifting dimensions,
appear only to reappear changed.

And the people, the people were inside,
gone to their rooms. The streets
& the air were gray & gritty
& I imagined myself drifting
over the bodies of those I've loved
or those I imagined I loved drifting
over their faces & hands until dawn came again
& the night was only a missing thing.

THE BLUE-EARED HOMUNCULUS
OF EXPECTATION

Cannot be tamed.
It is wild always,
bound to Exhaustion,
each a keeper & slave to the other.

They cannot see
the benefits of sitting alone
in a vineyard, or being with Landscape
until they are breathing it,
& so they dance with confusion,
hold hands with the clatter
that excess brings
& invade every absence.

Excitement alone is purpose.
Infants are taught this condition
from the beginning by well-meaning adults
who wish to entertain themselves
& believe they are communicating joy.

Some conditions cannot be cured.

COMMEMORATION OF A TONGUE

Facile switch, first fragment of happy thought
wedged in the slick saline of brimming ardor,
in meringue then, in shellfish bisque, Chablis,
or in any other, numbed between
with sorbet clemencies,
consumer of the living you earn
is pure sensation, wrapped around the premium
Honduran with Sumatra leaf, richest member
of the club, you have suffered a case of disaffection,

guest speaker for the moon,
and the high court justices,
reduced now to salt or spice, heat or cold,
dull, overworked, insensate,
like a verb of a forgotten language
left drying on a desert rock—
target of the heart, as for memories,
tongue, you should survive all others,
left alone, composed, entire, the only one.

TONGUE TO WARDS

to Catullus

You've awakened me once again,
old tool, I have no argument with you,
it is the bloody factory,
the automata of the corpus,
creatures of habit,
no other organ has my facility,
not lung or colon, not kidney
or pancreas, not even brain—
seat of mnemosyne, you are all
the same—speechless
& go about churning your acids,
pumping fluids, your functions
are yourselves in an ensemble
of self.

I do not need brain's word,
by conscience twisted,
only Instinct, to tell me
where to go & that is my companion
and my soul.

CONFESSION TO A GIRL

I want to become your life
because your future is all that is left.
It is what I was.
You are the subject of myself,
thus you represent everything.

If I am grief, I am my own memorial,
& see you by a wall of ivy talking
to a friend, or reading in a café,
or staring out at the rain listening
to music, the music of the world.

To you forever of the nineteenth year
I am jealous of your life just as I am
jealous of the lives of the dead.
I am the vampire of time,
voracious, I consume culture.
This is my Valentine & my sin.

THE GIRL'S REPLY

I have always found your admiration
attractive, but I think you act in haste.
You haven't considered everything.

There have been others, short-term affairs,
maybe you have suspected this.
Still, you remember me, after all.
And don't think I haven't noticed
how much you sound like me, as if I could love
you back to life again and again.

I've seen you watching me from a distance
like a timid voyeur dreaming
of what it would be like to take my heart.
Your intent is clear as day.

As for your age, it doesn't matter,
you are an exception—like me,
gods and days have their personalities
and I have mine—imagine me
going on like this, but I've been waiting
to go somewhere exotic

maybe a little extravagant. I am fluent
in French, but as I've said, I've been waiting
for you to say these things.
I want to hear them again.

OBSTRUCTION, A MONODY

This is not a moral tale.

The house on the hill
must be transparent
or it cannot be a house.

Perspective is obstruction.
It looms like the Colossus of Rhodes,
blocking new light,
or those cosmic giants, black holes,
feared devourers of Arion
containing unseen sylphides
of antimatter —the man-eating tree
of Madagascar—to swallow
unknown galaxies whole—

Without perspective art cannot be technique.

While monsters wrestle,

the house on the hill
must be transparent
if it is to be a house.

MYTHOS

Spring, & hummingbirds
whiz by the mollusk head,
creature of myself,
echo & air,
clumsy-hooved psyche,
heart of Wexford green,
by the rising of the moon,
outfitted for convenience,
in an appearance
that prances & cowers,
prates about the menagerie
with the accomplices of a plot,
a chain of deliquescent selves,
just as the hummingbirds arrive,
in circles broken by abrupt
distractions, when every observer retreats.

THE POLYMORPHS

The polymorph thinks multiply,
crawls & swims through elements
like PLATYPUS, but with a single
fixation & has shark-eye, a condition
necessary to preserve predation
also found in Chalma, the swamp dog,
& in the common roach, destroyer of worlds.

Monk Seal as Sea Devil,
Triton marinus, Historiae Animalium

ARS MEMORIA

Slender summer classic
what would you make of me?
Or what would you have me make of myself?

Something cold, I suppose, in stone
memorized until there was only the dark
face of an ancient moon.

ADDENDUM TO AN OPEN SESSION,

John Ashbery at the University of Arizona Museum of Art

The pecan trees near Picacho have arrived
along the Tucson highway, miles of them
crisscross the speeding fields on both sides
dividing space with form,
planted like an American Garden of Cyrus
where wandering among the rows was the attraction
then the scene shifted

to a prospect of flowers, five petals each,
yellow on the tan-print shirt, an early arrival
in the grand room of anonymous masters,
fourteenth or fifteenth-century Venetian
or Flemish, obscure and red figures
mingling on wood dark with moral themes,
here was pale Adam reclining
as Eve slipped, small shape of smoke
from his side, out of the womb of his lung,
the soft gray ground of the metrical grove,
prospects measured as from a gliding car—

you leaned forward for detail
then stepped back like a typical gallerian,
another departure, and here in the southwest,
where the weather is too warm & expectations
are labored, & from here you will depart
to your room & depart again . . . alternative
moments bunch up like little wombs of Adam.

Whatever we begin to do
becomes something else, turns away
from itself like a book or sign of the living,
subject to subject, the rows of images
in the grand room of anonymous masters.

But I began with the parallels of pecan trees,
that form of quincuncial planting lost
to antiquity, only to return to ask
what is the principle of departure,
from what conditions does it occur?

What is the agenda between these intervals
of longing? Tell us again how the morning
reclined across the landscape
when something was noticed
moving in the atmosphere
from this place to that, something that may
have wanted us here, the pattern of our arrivals,
visitors in a museum where the weather
was too warm, the expectations too severe,
and the masters, anonymous.

PURITY, A SYLPH

from Mythos

Not every poem can be successful.

When starting out, all references
to objects are stricken from the record.
No conventions, they are fraudulent.
No allusions, they are pretentious.
Go then Calliope & Minerva,
get off the page, & take with you
the poet who writes from the perspective
of satyr or owl.

It is the word & only the word
& in ensembles.

The book is more person than book.
On a shelf in the Regenstein
I am mind
until the days become scrambled
& unimaginable once again.

Here is clarity: when we were young,
twenty, a creature of ourselves,
& death, we knew, could occur
at any time and did not deserve
postponement, resistance,
or much attention.
It was simply—acceptable.

Perhaps we thought we would somehow
survive after all. We were our own fable.

The elaborate framework
for an elegant persuasion of another
world was unnecessary.
This one, with all its greatnesses,
& its death was all & all
was enough & enough
was purity.

STRANDED CAT

The cat in Lucien Clergue's *Eros and Thanatos*
lying on the beach at Sainte Marie-de-la-Mer
is only a half-decomposed corpse filled with sand.

The body resembles a piece of macabre iconography,
a stone *transi* with some fur still left along the spine,
down the striped tail curled like a long finger
as though to summon another image, here, it is
the photographer, Lucien, to make posthumous
meaning, a look, a life story—

She must have wandered out during low tide
pawing for shellfish on the sand bar and there
dallied too long, or in the lulling monotony
of the salty air, napped, and dreamt of crustacean
fantasies prancing past in improbable shapes
and floral colors. Her jaw, open and fixed

suggests she woke too late and cried to breathe
a final request, ignored, the oral cavity
holds the amber froth like a cup of champagne,
an offering for the anger of the sea, the sudden
tide, a coastal storm, an outburst, and the body
molded into the sand as though to deny

destruction, the rigid image of the thing,
a white eye, a necklace of foam, another
form that requires dissolution and absence,
the water becomes gentle as the hands of Antigone
in this moral dream of nature—itself dreaming
the personification of the scene by the shore—

so far as wind and water and sand agree
to focus in the production of being's text,
the burden of animation and the void
for an onlooker to accept these views, anger
alone, or benevolence to cancel the original image,
then all complaints are unjust and retracted—

The cat in Lucien Clergue's *Eros and Thanatos*
lying on the beach at Sainte Marie-de-la-Mer
is only a half-decomposed corpse filled with sand.

PREDICTABILITY

I look for returnings,
coming home to the same house
& learning it has not moved
in my absence,
the total agreement I have
with the family clock,
its soft gongs throughout the day,
(that has no sense of passage)
& the return of the seasons,
hard rain on the roof,
midnight dreams,
the certainty of night lights,
& how these things have not failed,
& the knowledge there are others
who are as I am, & that I am not
alone; there is always the desire
for the nameless, as if desire pursues
desire for its own sake,
& my human routines, dull as they are
to others, are things I count on,
the whirlwinds that arise
out of nowhere & make my concerns
nothing, along with every future,
& the imagination that tells me
there is such a thing as itself,
the assurance of good intentions
even tho' these may not turn out well,
& the daily expectation of something grand,
as if it, and monotony itself
were companions actually taking us somewhere.

RITES OF SPRING

Leave it for Poliziano to praise
   These figures from Ovid
   Gathered here in this betrayed Court
Of Botticelli's floating
   Only for the young who do not care
For the consequences of plenitude.

Leave it for them and this primavera,
   Swollen, open-mouthed, the smiling cheat struck
   Dumb with the expression of fecundity,
Why the whole party portends movement
   Toward their memorial Italian summer,
These who remain fixed in the postures of seduction.

  Please Father, let me spend the summer
    At Urbino . . .

  Like ignored contemporaries
     The voices of the children are long
        Down the halls
           And in the palace
              At Urbino there are volumes
                 Of light, why by the afternoon
                    The air is so thick I have seen
                       Small children float on staircases of it.

As clouds must move everyone is heading
   To the next season on the back of these panels
   The landscape is alive with dogs
Their faces twisted, pit bulls wild as Zephyrus,
   The dogs of caprice and contempt,
The cannibal dogs, *Connexio Rerum.*

To bite the thigh, devour the heart
   Of the virgin in the forest,
   Chloris stumbles pursued by the storm
And issues an endless inventory
   Of vines, a chain of cornflowers, gentians, roses
In *The Garden of The Dead*

Here are the leaves of the grape,
   The plant rooted in her heart,
   This too must be an ideal marriage
With the sign of the crow insatiable
   The storm dancing for light
      In the harmony of the memorial summer
         The dogs in the great rooms
            Barking at the sun.

GHOST CHOWS

Georgia O'Keeffe Returns to Abiquiú

Starkness, more or less, the sum of what was left here,
& slippers for the plaster floor thin as parchment,
strengthened with sheeps' blood.

The courtyard was quaint, and took my attention;
the thick walls, the penitentiary gate, it could be
my compound. Sagebrush covered the well,
and there was nothing else but white sand & white gravel,
a bit of wind & the taste of chalk dust.

Here the chows played. I see them now, groomed
by hands that were shapes themselves
making others, & weathered
river rock on shelves, brought home from the evening
walks with the dogs. They were the real protectors
all the time & never knew. The snakes & lions
were frightened off, or subdued.

The barren bedroom, as it was, a cell with a view,
one white cot with one white sheet,
a day bed in the studio, the same, a clinic,
more or less,
& outside, down the hill like a skirt,
was the bomb shelter.

*

Starkness, that was your accusation,
what I had not been in the early years,
but those were early years,
& what I had I had for others then,

& what I have I have now.

These mounds of color are similar,
or they are the same.

Juan, are you going out again?

The assistants, the friends, family, were wrong
to say I exhausted them, everyone,
it wasn't true. What I saw
were the signs of a self—it was mine—
in the silent motions of those forms,
these rooms, spaces, rock,
those great desert storms that came & went,
a nature of dramas, tearing itself
up again, over something troubling,
ruining one wardrobe or another. I wear black
These must be my forms again.

DESCRIPTION OF SEA LIFE

What was it, this crippled half-thing
sidling through thickness, an occasion
for being breathly frail, a glimpse

of an ancient image in an ancient sea,
one more servant in the urge of the world
to move toward something else as though its life
was spent trying to break the surface

where it could never survive alone
and still ascend, I see you ascend
a bridal dress, a headless subject
as though called by another buoy's bell

you would fold in my fist like a white heart,
filmy pump gathering old sea water,
you gather and disperse, gather to disperse
propelling yourself, an invalid organ

in the vital motion of the universe
of nettles, night nettles hundreds rising
through blue plasma, one turns, a medusan head
with cellular hair all in coils,

head or heart you were never the comparison
but the unknown expression about to speak
through the shape of watery human lips.

PSYCHOSIS

from Joseph Merrick

From my box of complaints,
memoranda of wrongs, I take
bits of paper, descriptions
of scorn, the names of those vandals
of wantonness, corrupt judges,
insatiable sadists, & pin them
to my mummy's rags
then go house to house,
like Halloween, my face wound
in bandages, a Psychosis
bumping its head against doors
even when they do not open,
& still I go on as if Compulsion
will correct Inequity,
not knowing why I should have any hope
of this, or what it is that stands hard behind
determination against futility.

NECESSITY

from Impulse, a Nymph

Necessity cannot live alone
& is created by other conditions

that are themselves created
by a central organizing authority,
an obligation seen in basic needs,
food, water, sex,
if exceeded, are poisonous,
& if neglected, the same.

Even a mother of invention
must have parents;
compulsion & delirium,
the pistons of celestial physics
& therein an epistemology
which is, above all, the lyric
& this is the new morality.

The lyric rests in locations,
& only appears during necessity's
lapse from its own tensions
as in meadows smeared
with yellow flowers,
or landscapes of Indian summers,
the balmy air where we counted
our youth & where there was no
other thing but the golden lens
& the ghost moon.

SELBSTMORD

Sylvia Plath
1932-1963

Something occurs with every act
that is beside the act,
that lingers like a phantom
over our decisions
made like bolted horses.

There was more to this than this.

More than vulgar act,
the abandoned children,
more than the flat
without light or heat, the pipes
broken in one of London's
coldest winters, more
than the hawkman walking toward Judea,
more than your fear made flesh,

or the casting away
of a life to punctuate a moment's art,
more than biographers say,
more than psychiatry's thinking,
or the stimulation of serotonin,
more than torment of mind,
or the runaway horses running still.

There is more to act than attribution.
There was the knowledge of slipping
into this world among so many
others that could have been,
that are now as we speak, but this one,
this one so rich with invitations—rustling
like spring trees—the anticipation

of the Great Work, the promise
of reunification, the wonderment of affection,
this one requiring obedience to the death notice
posted on the door through which all must enter:
von Anfang an und die Quelle.

It was spirit defiant, spirit resentful
of the necessity of humiliation & remorse.
It was your spirit angered
from the contract that reclaims everything,
yours from the insulted cosmos in you
from another world saying *nicht mehr,*
saying *dies nicht, dies nicht, dies nicht.*

JUSTICE

for Martin Turner

What are you but a mask of eloquent diction?
of colored print & papier-mâché?
But this is the world's wrapping,
& you, indentured to gratitude,
& gratitude is a loss to memory.

The drapes in the factory worker's home
prevent the view of the factory,
& the subtle fields with the affections
of warmth & color, trees & buds
cover the violence of magma,

it is the body's own organs covered
by flesh that permit any acceptance at all.
You are found in the clothing of the corpse,
arise from the suffering that is our own,
& from the suffering of others,

to become conscience & conceit.
The brass pole of the pole dancer
is spotted with thumb prints, body grease,
the film of human excrement.
And the derelict on the curb

or office manager, themselves a ruin
of pores, offensive secretions, could never
transcend themselves, and the other masks
to experience clarity, to glide
over the cemeteries of cities,
over inflatable street art, subways,
is unthinkable, but they do,
even in their ruin & the disintegration of flesh,
the mask itself, and this too
is in the equation of moral physics.

EARLY VIEWING

On The Death of The Father of Bibliography,
& Modern Zoology, Naturalist & Physician,
Belovéd Botanist, Conrad Gessner,
December 13, 1565, of the plague in Zürich

by Purity

MYTHOS & SATYR knock on the door three times,
(followed by three ominous drum beats in the background.)

Sylph Spectre appears, & leads the guests to his master's
chamber where he has asked to be taken to die
among his treasures; his seventy books, the walking stick
from Mt. Pilatus, stuffed Marmot & Porcupine,
other curiosities too strange to name,
his *Liber amicorum* with the signatures of 200
friends & fellow polyhistors with comments,
semi-completed illustrations of hundreds of plants,
a vase of dried tulips,
a letter from his father's brother, Andréas
thanking him for his contributions to the support
of his family, tho' he put himself in poverty
by his generosity, and among these things
there was a table with a linen mat,
a jar of ground licorice & comfry
for congestion, rose & sage for headache,
& lancets for bloodletting.

MYTHOS places his gift on the writing table with a folio on gems & minerals,
some notes for a book on insects.

—Yesterday afternoon when I first blistered , my patients brought this wreath—he points to his head—woven laurel of specimens—their physician is now the patient who cannot heal.

Purity steps forward:

> These blooms are from the family Gesneriad;
> African Violet & Flame Violet (*Episcia*)
> Lipsick plant (*Nematanthus*)
> Cape Primros (*Streptocarpus*)
> Cupid's Bower (*Achimenes*)

—This morning I boiled. Who knows what tomorrow will bring? In three days, return, & I will be gone.

—Stay any longer & you will contaminate yourselves. I will lock you out as I have the others. What is this you have brought?

MYTHOS & SATYR simultaneously: a collection of conditions.

Examining the gift—Every book is an orphanage, and every author an orphan. He puts in it the things he loves & wishes to protect.

Like you, Mythos, he is trying to find his family.

There is a commotion under the writing table. Confusion wrestles with Clarity. SATYR intervenes, but is overcome with remorse & seeks out a corner to whimper.

—Many seekers of knowledge study many things, but they do not study themselves, and therefore omit the subject which is the means & study of all study. But you, Mythos, have made yourself your subject.

Here Conrad extended his hand—As ennobled by Ferninand, & as his Supreme Polymath, I deem you, Mythos, Doctor of Dilettantes, & Prince of Arcana—

and thus Conrad gave him a wand of air so he would have dominion over the pastures of speculation—And further—he continued—I make you, Satyr, the companion of Mythos, to defend him in times of assault, for you are strong, where Mythos is weak in all but wandering among the dearness of things which so affect him.

—From now & forever hereafter you will search the world & all that may follow for the new & curious, so you may record them & they will not be lost, & others may know, tho' they may not marvel at them as they do the polymorph. May your experiences serve to occupy the expanding void.

To do this you must at all times avoid fraud & predation that will surround you while among men, & fix yourselves on your experiences in the natural world, and those of your imaginings for they are creations also and are no less than other creatures. I see endless fields for new plants & animals, of things not yet known, and many are empty still to our vision, and yes, Mythos even among these, wondrous as they are, is still a place for others. Wrap yourselves in their lyrics.

We are called to fill the unfillable.

Remember, as you go, the animals are our first tutors.
The she-wolf vicious in anger (*de ira*) will care
for the forsaken human infant even more than its own mother—
this cannot be the best of worlds—

And when he had trouble breathing, asked
for the elixir Oxymel, he once described
to Occo for his pharmacopoeia as treatment
for asthma, & then another . . . then lapsed
from sleep to wakefulness . . . to sleep again.

And that was how Mythos & Satyr became indivisible,
sent to catalogue the creations of themselves,
& all new forms that stuck their imaginings,
& about midnight, after they departed
on their journey, having stayed with the polymath
for nearly three days, about midnight, when all remedies failed,
when the poultices were removed, the vinegar
to clean the lesions stood on the stand, Conrad,
his notebook & pencil at his side, at midnight,
passed into the source of purity,
or into something he could not know,
but as a glance, or into the invisible arms
of a holy family having professed his faith
to the theologian Bullinger, or into the great concurring
pinwheels of the cosmos, or into nothing at all,
& his wife, in disbelief, stared & stared.

Monster Carp, Conrad Gessner, 1563.

GUIDE
TO CARE
& FEEDING

The Great Boas, Devouring Child, 1558.

GIFTS

Nature overcompensates:
the dicephalics, for instance,
or those additional vertebrae,
surplus molars, extra digits,
one more finger or toe
just for good measure, and here,
here is another five-chambered heart.

As if there is never enough,
like the patients of good will
who cannot bring enough red wine,
garlic necklaces, daily calendars
with inspirational quotations
given from gratitude,
or admiration, or from the one
last and only hope

they bring other things,
they bring themselves.

It is the excess of the well intentioned,
the camping outfitter who overfits,
the granger who overfeeds
for a winter that will never come.
The effusions of a heart pumping wildly
behind the heart, with more imagination
than any body can bear.

HIGH NOON AT THE STANLEY

There has been discord traveling
through the mountains
in midsummer, my son
remains in the car, fourteen and angered
by everything. I have crossed
the wide lawn of sculptured light
through the heavy domes of clouds
to a table on the grand porch
with its fluted columns, gold acanthus leaves.

My wife walks the grounds to collect her mind.
The boy is off with a camera to find elk.
We have arrived by troubled coincidence
& exhaustion. Every state has something
like this, a refuge at higher elevations.
Hummingbirds arrive. I consider the menu,
Poached salmon, white wine.

Estes Park, a postcard vista, layers
of blue hills falling away into mist,
quiet news of a summer shower later
out on the mountain roads.

My family has been away long enough
I have found time
for a few lines of my own.
The architecture of this hotel
is the architecture of language itself,
a solace of structure, wood & sun,
& all that is outside of this
is the confusion that fails the mind.

The prosperous converse on the lawn,
the best of their day, discussing things,
while their replacements, the student waiters
in white aprons & black ties share plans
for the weekend, as the far trees move
on those blue hills, as those hills themselves move
toward all that is accepted, like Roman stoics
in the light that is hard & cold,
where the best tutors of the speechless live,
where the truly good cannot be tragic.

AN GORTA MOR

What is poetry but a mouth,
open & empty like the great hunger,
a mouth with green lips,
stains of vegetation.

WHEN IN THE LASTING LOVELINESS OF THINGS

When night calls and you are not to be found,
and when evening stops its descent and is still,
as if waiting for you to appear
before it falls into night once again,

When no thing will turn, not leaves or lovers
in the park, or arise, not breeze or bird,
when these things are still, and waiting for your
return, as if they should never move again

Without you, and when I call and call your name
down the empty streets, lined with winter trees,
when all forms have ceased for the sight of you,
for you to arrive and make them possible again—

I have lived my life for this, mine and yours,
in this moment, always before nightfall.

THE DOORS OF DUBLIN

The doors of Dublin are Georgian doors,
those facing St. Stephen's Green, heavy and wide
and up cold cement steps, each with a brass knocker,
the head of some shining, splendid mythic beast,
Circe, or Siren, or David, or Lion-about-to-speak,
always a single color, solid and bright,
say warm heart-red with white-trimmed fanlight,
night-sky blue, Cobalt-dawn, or Kelly green
set in coarsest stone like Dubliners themselves.

OTHER ACTS

After the carnivorous business
was completed out on the savannah
or in elegant suburban bedrooms,
after this, all this
memory forgot, forgave itself once more
as though wantonness & other acts
were sudden rends, small distortions
to say this never really occurred,
to conceal a family disagreement
so the other conversation could continue
like a pair of lovers among ruins
on a wine-colored evening
when all is agreeable & everything
said is certain.

AFTER HOURS,
A CONSOLATION

from Plenitude

That we should not regret the world
for what it was, or seemed to be,
because it did not disclose itself
enough to us, or that our verses
& our lives failed us, that once
we found the one perfect thing,
a romantic moment, somewhere
say in the rain one afternoon
& have sought its return ever since
& regret our yearning as much
as the thing lost, until we wonder
if it was ever as perfect
as we once thought, or worse,
more than we imagined,
until all things eventually reach
their mutual goal & become
a cancellation, or diffuse
by recombining into a mass
that cannot cease from growing,
until then, we will not
make an oath, or place a claim
on any living thing so some breath
may outlast us, ourselves,
& all those things about us.

Nota Bene: On the cover images & how the Hyena imitates the voices of shepherds—

The Beaver (Castor) . . . is gentle; its testicles are highly suitable for medicine. Physiologus says of it that, when it knows a hunter is pursuing it, it bites off its testicles and throws them in the hunter's face and, taking flight, escapes. But if another hunter is in pursuit, the Beaver rears up and displays its sexual organs. When the hunter sees it lacks testicles, he leaves it alone.

The Panther . . . has only the Dragon as its enemy . . . and from its mouth comes a very sweet odour, as if it were a mixture of every perfume. When other animals hear its voice, they follow wherever it goes . . . only the Dragon, hearing its voice, is seized by fear and flees into the caves beneath the earth. There, unable to bear the scent, it grows numbed within itself and remains motionless, as if dead. Thus our Lord Jesus Christ, the true Panther, descending from Heaven, snatched us from the power of the devil . . .

The hyena should not be eaten because it is dirty and has two natures, male and female. Both sexual organs are clearly shown. It dwells in the tombs of the dead and devours human bodies. Its spine is rigid and it must move its whole body in order to turn. Solinus recounts many marvelous things about the hyena. First, it stalks the sheepfolds of shepherds and circles their houses by night, and by listening carefully learns their speech, so that it can imitate the human voice, in order to fall on any man whom it has lured out at night. The hyena also [imitates] human vomit and devours the dogs it has enticed with faked sounds of retching. If dogs hunting the hyena accidentally touch its shadow behind, they lose their voices and cannot bark. In its search for buried bodies, the hyena digs up graves.

from *The Aberdeen Bestiary*

Poems of Michael Gessner have been nominated for a Pushcart Prize and as finalists for "Discovery"/*The Nation*, and the Pablo Neruda Award. *Beast Book* is his fourth poetry title. His work has been featured in *American Letters & Commentary, American Literary Review, The Journal of The American Medical Association, Oxford Magazine*, and others. He has read at University College Dublin, and the American-Irish Historical Society (NYC.) His work has been called "Striking," (David Barber, *The Atlantic*,) and "Structurally ingenious," (Jonathan Galassi, Farrar, Straus & Giroux.) He lives in Tucson.

Made in the USA
Charleston, SC
20 August 2010